The Making of the Middle East

The Palestine Mandate
and the
Creation of Israel
1920-1949

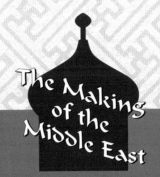

The Making of the Middle East

The Palestine Mandate
and the
Creation of Israel
1920-1949

Alan H. Luxenberg

Mason Crest Publishers
Philadelphia

Frontispiece: The state of Israel declared its independence in May 1948.

Produced by OTTN Publishing, Stockton, N.J.

Mason Crest Publishers
370 Reed Road
Broomall, PA 19008
www.masoncrest.com

First printing

1 3 5 7 9 8 6 4 2

Library of Congress Cataloging-in-Publication Data

Luxenberg, Alan H.
   The Palestine mandate and the creation of Israel, 1920-1949 / Alan H. Luxenberg.
      p. cm. — (The making of the Middle East)
   Includes bibliographical references and index.
   ISBN-13: 978-1-4222-0170-1
   ISBN-10: 1-4222-0170-8
   1. Jewish-Arab relations—Juvenile literature. I. Title.
   DS119.7.L79 2008
   956.94'04—dc22

                              2007024684

Table of Contents

Introduction:
The Importance of the Middle East

The region known as the Middle East has a significant impact on world affairs. The countries of the greater Middle East—the Arab states of the Arabian Peninsula, Eastern Mediterranean, and North Africa, along with Israel, Turkey, Iran, and Afghanistan—possess a large portion of the world's oil, a valuable commodity that is the key to modern economies. The region also gave birth to three of the world's major faiths: Judaism, Christianity, and Islam.

In recent years it has become obvious that events in the Middle East affect the security and prosperity of the rest of the world. But although such issues as the wars in Iraq and Afghanistan, the floundering Israeli-Palestinian peace process, and the struggles within countries like Lebanon and Sudan are often in the news, few Americans understand the turbulent history of this region.

Human civilization in the Middle East dates back more than 8,000 years, but in many cases the modern conflicts and issues in the region can be attributed to events and decisions made during the past 150 years. In particular, after World War I ended in 1918, the victorious Allies—especially France and Great Britain—redrew the map of the Middle East, creating a number of new countries, such as Iraq, Jordan, and Syria. Other states, such as Egypt and Iran, were dominated by foreign powers until after the Second World War. Many of the Middle Eastern countries did not become independent until the 1960s or 1970s. Political and economic developments in the Middle Eastern states over the past four decades have shaped the region's direction and led to today's headlines.

The purpose of the MAKING OF THE MIDDLE EAST series is to nurture a better understanding of this critical region, by providing the basic history along

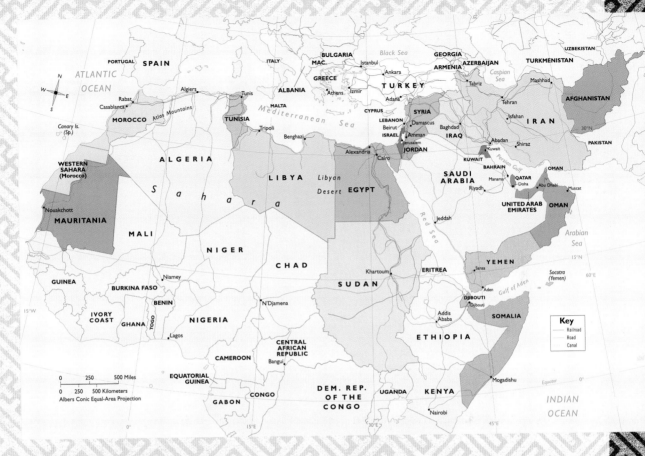

Key
— Railroad
— Road
— Canal

with explanation and analysis of trends, decisions, and events. Books will examine important movements in the Middle East, such as the development of nationalism in the 1880s and the rise of Islamism from the 1970s to the present day.

The 10 volumes in the MAKING OF THE MIDDLE EAST series are written in clear, accessible prose and are illustrated with numerous historical photos and maps. The series should spark students' interest, providing future decision-makers with a solid foundation for understanding an area of critical importance to the United States and the world.

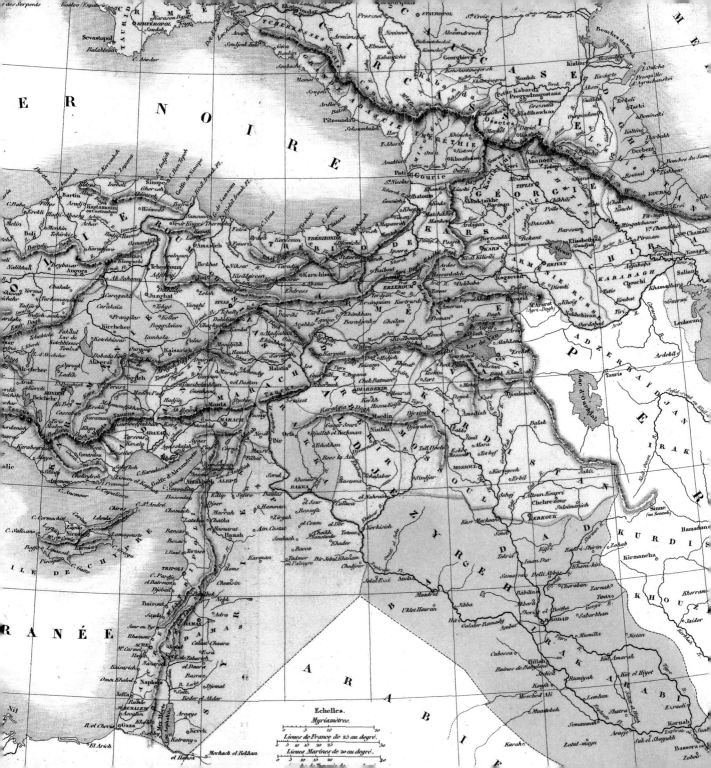

(Opposite) This map of the Ottoman Empire, circa 1870, shows some of the areas ruled by the empire including the Eastern Mediterranean. (Right) A Jewish man prays at the Western Wall, part of the retaining wall of the ancient Jewish Temple in Jerusalem, which was destroyed by the Romans in 70 C.E.

1 *A Jewish State for the Jewish Nation*

*P*eople often use the terms "state" and "nation" interchangeably. However, these two words can have distinctly different meanings, and it is important to understand the difference between them when studying the history of the Middle East, and particularly of Israel. To put it simply, a *state* is the political apparatus that governs a country, while a *nation* is a group of people who share a cultural heritage and a set of beliefs. Nationalism is the idea that a nation should have its own state.

The state of Israel was established in 1948, yet the story of the Jewish nation is 4,000 years old. It is the tale of a people who, despite being expelled from their homeland nearly 2,000 years ago and being persecuted throughout the world ever since, managed not only to survive as a people but to return to their ancient homeland to establish a modern, democratic state.

"In the Beginning..."

In the Bible, the story of the Jewish people begins with Abraham (circa 1800 B.C.E.), who left his home in Ur in Mesopotamia (modern-day Iraq) to settle in the land of Canaan (modern-day Israel). In Jewish tradition, it was Abraham who first received God's promise to give the land of Canaan to his descen-

The story of the Jewish people is told in the Five Books of Moses, which the Jews call their Torah. Christians recognize the same scriptures as the Old Testament of the Bible. Muslims recognize Moses, whom they call Musa, as one prophet in a line of prophets that includes Jesus and Muhammad. Throughout the Torah, God promises the land of Canaan (roughly corresponding to Israel) to the Jewish people.

dants, the "Children of Israel"; that promise was repeated to other prophets named in the Bible.

Around the year 1000 B.C.E. King David is said to have united the Israelites into a powerful kingdom. For most of the next millennium, Jews either ruled over the land themselves or enjoyed some measure of autonomy under foreign rule.

In 63 B.C.E. the Jewish kingdom of Judea (which is what the land was then called, and from which name the word "Jew" is derived) became a province of the Roman Empire. Although Judea had some degree of autonomy, revolts by the Jews against Roman rule were common. After putting down a revolt led by Simon Bar Kokbha in 135 C.E., Roman authorities outlawed the Jewish religion and expelled nearly all of the Jews from Judea. They renamed the land Palestina (in English, Palestine). As a result of Roman rule, the Jews were scattered to other parts of the world, though the Jews retained a small presence in Palestine throughout the subsequent centuries.

The Interest of Other Faiths

In 325 C.E. the Roman Emperor Constantine made Christianity, a religion that had originated in Judea, a legal religion in the empire. By the end of the fourth century, Christianity was the official religion of the Roman Empire, which stretched from the British Isles to Asia Minor and included North Africa and the Middle East. Because Palestine had been the home of Jesus, it held a special place to Christians.

In 395 the Roman Empire was divided into two parts. Rome was the principal city of the western empire, while Constantinople (now Istanbul,

This Roman-era mosaic showing early Christian symbols—fish and bread with crosses—was found in a home in Jerusalem. Because Jesus Christ was crucified in Jerusalem, Christians have a special reverence for the ancient city.

Turkey) was the capital of the eastern empire. The western empire was the weaker of the two, and it collapsed in the late fifth century. The eastern empire, which included wealthy provinces like Egypt, Syria, Palestine, and the cities of Asia Minor, lasted for almost 1,000 years as the Byzantine Empire.

During the early years of the seventh century a man named Muhammad began preaching a new religion, Islam, on the Arabian Peninsula. Once the

Prophet Muhammad united the Arabs under his new religion, Muslim armies emerged from the peninsula to conquer much of the Middle East, southern Europe, and South Asia. By 634 the Arabs had seized Palestine from the Byzantine Empire.

In the late seventh century the Dome of the Rock was built over the spot where, according to Islamic tradition, the Prophet Muhammad ascended into heaven. The shrine is built on the foundation of the ancient Jewish Temple of Jerusalem.

Between 634 and 1917 Palestine was part of 10 different Muslim empires, interrupted by 200 years of rule by Christian European crusaders. During the entire period of Muslim rule, Palestine never existed as an independent political entity or even as a unified administrative unit. It was an area ruled by empires based in Baghdad or Damascus or Cairo or Constantinople.

Jerusalem held importance not only for the Jews but also for Muslims and Christians. Jesus had preached in Jerusalem, and it was just outside the city that Roman authorities crucified him, nailing him to a wooden cross. The Muslims built the Dome of the Rock and the Al Aqsa Mosque on the spot where the Jewish temple had once stood; according to Muslim tradition, the Prophet Muhammad had ascended to heaven from this spot to speak with Moses, Jesus, and others whom Muslims consider messengers. Thus did Jerusalem become a city revered by people of three faiths.

The Diaspora

Though a small number of Jews remained in Palestine, after 135 C.E. most were scattered to other parts of the world. When a group of people lives outside their homeland, they are said to live in the diaspora. Life in the diaspora was not easy for the Jews. They were persecuted in most of Christian Europe for over a thousand years. Often Jews were forced to convert to Christianity or be expelled from their homes or killed. Lies were spread about the Jews in medieval Europe, accusing them of killing Christian children so that they could consume the blood in a bizarre ritual. During the 14th, 15th, and 16th centuries Jews were forced to leave countries like Spain, France, and England. In Spain, the expulsion of Jews—the culmination of the

Inquisition—was undertaken in 1492, the same year that Christopher Columbus sailed to the New World under the Spanish flag. The Jews would not be allowed to return for hundreds of years.

During the diaspora Jews around the world included *Eretz Yisrael* (Hebrew for "Land of Israel") in their daily prayers. The destruction of the First Temple in Jerusalem in 586 B.C.E. by Babylonians and the destruction of the Second Temple in 73 C.E. by the Romans were also mourned by Jews everywhere during the somber annual holiday of Tisha B'Av. Jews even recall the destruction of the temples during their wedding ceremonies, when the groom crushes a glass at the conclusion of the ceremony. To this day, the Western Wall, a remnant of the retaining wall of the Temple, is a holy site visited by thousands of Jews around the world every year. These are just a few examples of the ancient connection between the Jewish people, the land of Israel, and its capital in Jerusalem.

By the 19th century Jews were finally granted full citizenship in the countries of Western Europe. However, most of the world's Jews lived in Eastern Europe and in the Russian Empire, where they were subjected to violent pogroms (government-encouraged mob violence targeted at Jewish communities). While small groups of Jews had migrated to the ancient homeland in Palestine, these moves had always been religiously inspired. In the late 19th century, however, dire conditions in the Russian empire led to more organized and more political efforts.

Beginning in the 1800s the Jews of Eastern Europe started talking seriously about returning to their ancient homeland, seeing it as a "promised land" where they would be free from persecution. The first of five Jewish

A group of murdered Jews are laid out after a pogrom in Russia, circa 1900. Riots and violence against Jews were common in Russia and other parts of Eastern Europe during the late 19th and early 20th century.

immigration movements to Palestine, called *aliyahs* in Hebrew, began in 1882. In contrast, the Jews of Western Europe wanted, for the most part, nothing more than to fit in to the societies in which they lived. The idea of returning to an ancient homeland seemed undesirable to them.

The Modern Zionist Movement Forms

One secular (non-religious) Jew from Vienna changed all that. Theodor Herzl is considered the father of modern Zionism—the movement to create a State of Israel. Herzl had been a journalist covering the trial of Captain Alfred Dreyfus in Paris in 1893. Dreyfus, a Jewish captain in the French military, was falsely accused of treason, and when Herzl witnessed the mobs outside the courtroom with posters reading "Death to the Jews," he sensed that Jews had no future in Europe. France at that time was the most liberal and tolerant country in Europe, and if its people held such attitudes toward Jews then their future in Europe appeared dim.

In 1896 Herzl wrote a book called *The Jewish State*, in which he argued that for their own security and well-being the Jewish nation needed its own country, where Jews could make the rules and operate the government—just as other nationalities had formed states in modern Europe. The next year he convened the first World Zionist Congress in Basle, Switzerland. Its purpose was to organize Jewish leaders to work toward creating the Jewish state.

Herzl tried to secure international support for a Jewish state, beginning with Imperial Germany, but he made the deepest impact in Britain. Herzl was willing to consider the British suggestion of establishing a temporary Jewish homeland in Uganda, an area in Africa then under British colonial control. But the preponderance of people in the Zionist movement felt there was only one possible territory for the Jews, and that was Eretz Yisrael.

Theodor Herzl (1860–1904) was a Jewish journalist who lived in the Austro-Hungarian Empire. Disturbed by anti-Semitism in Europe, Herzl founded the modern Zionist movement and worked toward the establishment of a Jewish homeland.

The problem was that since 1517 the land had been controlled by the Ottoman Empire, a powerful Muslim empire that ruled parts of the Middle East, North Africa, and Western Asia. The Ottoman ruler was both a political and spiritual leader of the Muslim world, and had no interest in establishing a Jewish homeland. Although a small number of Jews were permitted to move into the area between 1882 and 1914, neither Herzl nor his successors (Herzl died in 1904) could persuade the Ottoman sultan to allow large-scale immigration.

War Affects Palestine's Future

In August 1914 the First World War began in Europe. The Ottoman Empire soon aligned itself with the Central Powers (Germany and Austria-Hungary), which were fighting against Britain, France, and Russia. Eventually, Italy and the United States joined the Allies in the war against the Central Powers.

To help win the war, British leaders made promises to many different groups of people. One group was the Arabs, who were Ottoman subjects. One Arab leader approached by the British was Sharif Hussein, who ruled a coastal strip of the Arabian Peninsula (the Hejaz) and served as guardian of the Muslim holy sites in Mecca and Medina. Hussein possessed great ambitions, seeking to replace Ottoman rule over Arabia with an empire of his own. With British assistance, he thought he might succeed.

There was no formal agreement between the British and Sharif Hussein, but understandings were laid out in a series of 10 letters between the sharif and Sir Henry McMahon, the British High Commissioner in Egypt. The Hussein-

McMahon correspondence (1915–1916) promised independence for the Arabs under Hussein's rule in exchange for his leading an Arab revolt against the Ottoman Turks.

But the British were secretly making other plans for the region at the same time. In 1916 French and British diplomats made a secret pact known as the Sykes-Picot Agreement. This was a plan for the postwar division of Ottoman territories in the Middle East into British and French "spheres of influence." A third plan became public in November 1917, when a letter from British Foreign Secretary Arthur James Balfour declared Britain's support for the establishment of a "national home" for Jews in Palestine.

In the view of many, all of these agreements or understandings were contradictory, offering the same land to Arabs, Jews, and the European powers and leading some observers to call Palestine "the thrice promised land." Others argue that the agreements were deliberately imprecise about borders,

The Balfour Declaration
November 2, 1917

"His Majesty's Government view with favour the establishment in Palestine of a national home for the Jewish people, and will use their best endeavours to facilitate the achievement of this object, it being clearly understood that nothing shall be done which may prejudice the civil and religious rights of existing non-Jewish communities in Palestine, or the rights and political status enjoyed by Jews in any other country."

British authorities declare martial law after capturing Jerusalem from the Ottoman Empire in December 1917. After the First World War, the British maintained a military presence in Palestine.

so while the claimants on the land may have had conflicting claims, the promises made to them were not necessarily conflicting. Ultimately, Britain tried to make good on all its promises, though it was never able to satisfy the competing claimants. It did defer to the French in Syria and Lebanon, it did foster the creation of independent Arab states, and it did carve out a space for a Jewish homeland.

The Mandates Are Enacted

After an armistice was signed halting the fighting in the First World War, the victorious Allied powers met in Paris to discuss the terms of the peace treaty that would officially end the conflict. At the urging of U.S. President Woodrow Wilson, the delegates to the 1919 Paris Peace Conference agreed to form an international organization called the League of Nations (a precursor to the United Nations). The League was intended as a deliberative assembly in which nations could settle their disagreements through diplomacy and negotiation, without having to resort to war.

One of the most important tasks faced by the Allied leaders at the Paris Peace Conference—particularly the "Big Four": Wilson, British Prime Minister David Lloyd George, French Prime Minister Georges Clemenceau, and Italian Prime Minister Vittorio Orlando—was to determine the future of territories once controlled by the defeated Central Powers. In a speech in January 1918, Wilson had proposed terms on which a permanent peace could be based. Wilson's "14 Points" called for independence for nationalities that had been living under Ottoman or Austro-Hungarian rule for centuries. The 12th point referred specifically to the disposition of the Ottoman territories:

> The Turkish portions of the present Ottoman Empire should be assured a secure sovereignty, but the other nationalities which are now under Turkish rule should be assured an undoubted security of life and an absolutely unmolested opportunity of an autonomous development.

The Arabs, Jews, Kurds, Armenians, and other nationalities living in the Ottoman Empire understood Wilson to mean that they should gain their own independent nation-states after the war. However, although the Allies did create a number of new countries during and after the Paris Peace Conference, most were not granted full independence. Instead, the League of Nations—which was dominated by Britain and France—developed a system by which the major powers would oversee the affairs of these new states, helping them to establish good governments and social institutions before they became independent. The system of mandates was devised to provide an orderly way for dependent territories to assume the responsibilities of self-government while protecting the interests of the victorious powers in the Middle East. Many people living in these "mandate states" did not like this arrangement, however, believing the mandate system was simply a way that the colonial powers of Europe could continue to exploit the resources of their lands.

In April 1920 Allied representatives met in San Remo, Italy, to determine the disposition of the former Ottoman territories. The northern half of the Ottoman province of Syria was assigned to France as the French Mandates of Syria and Lebanon. The southern half, which included the modern states of Israel and Jordan, as well as the areas known as the West Bank and Gaza, became the British Mandate for Palestine. Three Ottoman *vilayets* (districts)—

Allied leaders (left to right) David Lloyd George, Vittorio Orlando, Georges Clemenceau, and Woodrow Wilson meet outside a hotel in Paris during the 1919 peace conference. Arab and Jewish leaders were disappointed at the Paris Peace Conference when they did not receive the independent states that each believed they had been promised during the war.

Mosul, Baghdad, and Basra—were combined to create a new state, Iraq, which was also a British mandate. Britain and France took on the authority and responsibility for managing their mandated territories, supposedly with the interests of the inhabitants in mind.

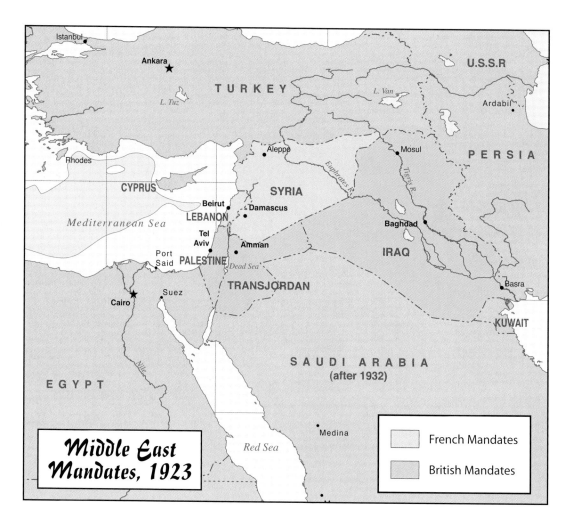

Middle East Mandates, 1923

Legend:
- French Mandates
- British Mandates

In the case of the British, their primary interests in the Middle East had to with protecting access to their prize colony, India, via the Suez Canal, as well as to oil resources. But the British government had other reasons for its interest in Palestine. There had been a tradition of Christian Zionism going back to 19th century Britain. It was the Christian Zionist Lord Shaftesbury who in 1853 had coined a famous phrase describing Palestine as "a land without a people for a people without a land." He did not mean that the land had no people living in it; he meant that there were no people living there who defined themselves as a "people" or "nation." The people living there thought of themselves as Muslims, or as subjects of the Ottoman Empire, or as Syrians because Palestine was considered by many as southern Syria, or as members of a particular family or clan. But the idea of a "Palestinian" did not yet exist. As for the other half of the phrase, the Christian Zionists were keen to acknowledge Christianity's role in persecuting the Jews, and wished to make up for it by giving Jews a land they could call their own.

When Britain took possession of Palestine from the Ottomans in December 1917, it was not even a single province but a collection of *sanjaks*, or sub-provinces. The land was mostly desert, its marshes infested with malaria-carrying insects, and the remaining good land was owned by a few wealthy landowners who resided in other parts of the Arab world. The people were impoverished, and the population was little more than half a million. Most residents of Palestine were Muslims, and they did not wish to accept Jewish immigration into the region on a massive scale or permit the emergence of a Jewish state in which Muslims might one day become a minority.

(Opposite) This colored postcard shows a Palestinian Arab farmer using a simple wooden plow to till the soil. When this picture was taken around 1900, most residents of Palestine were still using agricultural methods that dated back thousands of years. (Right) The Jewish settlement at Tel Aviv, circa 1930.

2 The Two Nations of Palestine

When the General Syrian Congress and the major Palestinian organizations met in 1919 and 1920, all demanded that Palestine (or Southern Syria, as it was called) remain part of Syria. Syrians considered Palestine (and the territories corresponding to the modern states of Lebanon and Jordan) to be part of Syria. This sentiment existed for a long time after the establishment of the Syrian Arab Republic in 1946 and the State of Israel in 1948. (Historically, Syria itself had never been an independent political entity but simply part of one empire or another.)

Palestinian Nationalism Emerges

It was also around 1920 that Palestinian nationalism emerged for the first time. Palestinian nationalism was largely a response to the growing Jewish presence in Palestine and to the Arab fear that the Jewish presence would eventually lead to Jewish rule over the area. As early as April 1920 there were signs of growing Palestinian restiveness in the form of Arab riots against Jewish settlements, resulting in the deaths of 46 Jews.

But the trigger was the French ouster of Syria's King Faisal (son of Britain's World War I ally, Sharif Hussein of Mecca) in July 1920. In March the General Syrian Congress had elected Faisal king of a united Syria (which included Palestine, Lebanon, and Jordan). However, the League of Nations established several mandate states from this territory, and the French forced Faisal out in order to assert their control over the Syrian mandate.

With the dream of Greater Syria in ruins, the aspirations of the Arabs of Palestine turned in a different direction—for an independent Palestine that they would rule. Once Palestinian Arabs began to think of themselves as a unified people—a nation—there were two nations living within the confines of Palestine, both hoping to achieve sovereignty over the entire area of what is often called "historic Palestine."

The boundaries that make up "historic Palestine" do not actually go back all that far in time. The borders were drawn by the British and French after World War I. Before then, the boundaries were somewhat arbitrary and often changed. The last time there was a distinct entity in that area was during the time of the Crusaders (1099–1291), when part of the land was called the Latin Kingdom of Jerusalem. During the 1920 peace conference, Palestine's boundaries were the subject of heated discussion. British Prime Minister David Lloyd George is said to have referred the other delegates to the work of Reverend George Adam Smith, whose book *Historical Geography of the Holy Land* (1901) was considered the authoritative text on the subject.

The British Mandate

In July 1920 Britain ended its military administration of the territory and appointed its first High Commissioner in Palestine, Sir Herbert Samuel. He sought to cultivate the development of representative institutions in Palestine through a legislative council that would consist of Muslim, Christian, and Jewish representatives. He also established an Arab Agency on the model of the Jewish Agency, an organization that was already deeply involved in representing the needs and interests of the Jewish

Sir Herbert Samuel (right) was the first British High Commissioner in Palestine. In this 1925 photo, he is standing with Field Marshal Edmund Allenby (left), who commanded the British troops that captured Palestine during the First World War, and Lord Arthur Balfour, who as Britain's foreign secretary issued the Balfour Declaration in 1917.

community. However, not wishing to grant any legitimacy to the Mandatory government, the Arabs decided not to participate.

Ironically, by trying to inhibit the development of representative government institutions in Palestine, the Arabs were actually aiding the interests of the Jews. The demographic imbalance between Arabs (88 percent of the population) and Jews (12 percent) meant that if the Arabs had participated in a democratic government, Jewish immigration would inevitably have been curtailed and the Zionist plan for an independent state stalled.

In May 1921 there was an outbreak of Arab hostilities against Jews, this time in Jaffa, resulting in the deaths of 48 Arabs and 47 Jews. As a result, the British High Commissioner Herbert Samuel temporarily suspended Jewish immigration, hoping to allay Arab fears of Jewish domination and thereby defuse the hostile atmosphere.

On July 24, 1922, the League of Nations confirmed the assignment of the Palestine Mandate to Great Britain, tasking it specifically with the responsibility of putting into effect the terms of the Balfour Declaration. Great Britain, the resolution said, "shall be responsible for placing the country [Palestine] under such political, administrative and economic conditions as will secure the establishment of the Jewish national home." At the same time, Britain was to safeguard "the civil and religious rights of all the inhabitants of Palestine," a sentiment that also echoed the text of the Balfour Declaration. Thus was the Balfour Declaration—and the goal of establishing a Jewish national home in Palestine—made part of an international agreement.

However, the League of Nations also agreed to allow Great Britain to withhold application of these provisions of the mandate in the area east of the Jordan River (the West Bank), which made up about 78 percent of the territory. Subsequently, Britain established the Emirate of Transjordan in this area. The territory west of the Jordan River, which became known as the Palestine Mandate, constituted 22 percent of the total British mandated territories in the region. A son of Sharif Hussein named Abdullah was named emir of Transjordan, which like Palestine was also under British mandate. The British Mandate period officially began on September 29, 1923.

Jews Immigrate to Palestine

If one great boost to Jewish immigration into Palestine was the pogroms in the Russian empire in the late 1800s and early 1900s, another great boost was the 1924 Johnson Law limiting immigration into the United States. The vast majority of Russian and East European Jews had fled to other parts of Europe and the United States rather than to Palestine. Now the door to the United States was closing, so growing numbers of Jews emigrated to Palestine.

Jewish immigrants developed the land and enlarged the economy. They hoped that by contributing to the well-being of all the land's inhabitants they could pave the way for Jewish-Arab conciliation. Arabs from surrounding areas began moving to Palestine because of the growing opportunity there. There had been signs that Arab-Jewish conciliation was not an impossible vision, such as the 1919 agreement between Syrian King Faisal and the Zionist leader Chaim Weizmann to cooperate on the development of a Jewish National Homeland. However, this agreement had collapsed when Faisal failed to achieve his larger goals with respect to Syria.

But the Arabs in Palestine did not see the Jews as people returning to an ancestral homeland; they saw them as Westerners colonizing land that belonged to them. And the idea of a Jewish state conflicted with the experiences of over a thousand years in which Christians and Jews had a protected but second-class status (called *dhimmi*) under Muslim rule in the Middle East.

To protest Jewish immigration into Palestine, the Arab residents of the region frequently resorted to violence. This is an anti-Zionist demonstration at Jerusalem's Damascus gate, March 1920.

British troops search pedestrians for weapons after a riot in Palestine, November 1921.

The idea that Jews might rule over land that Muslims had ruled for 1,300 years was humiliating to the Muslims.

Immigration Rises and Falls

In 1922, as a result of increasing Arab agitation, the British released the first of several official "White Papers," or statements of policy, with respect to the

Palestine Mandate. The 1922 White Paper, known as the Churchill White Paper for then Colonial Secretary in the Ministry of Foreign Affairs Winston Churchill, hoped to alleviate some of the agitation by clarifying the British position. A Jewish homeland did not imply a Jewish state, said the paper, and only as many Jews would be allowed in as could reasonably be expected to add rather than detract from the economic resources of Palestine. Thus, for the first time, limits on Jewish immigration were envisaged. Moreover, instead of a Jewish state, the paper envisaged a "binational" state in which Jews and Arabs would govern together. At the same time, however, the paper insisted that Jews had a right to live in Palestine.

During the 1920s immigration slowed down anyway, and as a result so did the agitation. But differences over the Western Wall in Jerusalem triggered new Arab riots against the Jews in 1929, including a massacre in the city of Hebron, where a Jewish settlement had existed for thousands of years. Once again, an official British government report, the Hope-Simpson Report, recommended a cessation of Jewish immigration. Simultaneously, the Passfield White Paper was issued, proposing restrictions on Jewish immigration as well as the termination of Jewish land purchases. This was reversed by a new British government that came to power shortly thereafter, and indeed in response to an ever worsening situation in Germany and central Europe, Jewish immigration into Palestine increased dramatically in the 1930s. This in turn increased tensions between Palestinian Arabs and the Jews, on the one hand, and Palestinian Arabs and the British, on the other, giving rise to a new Arab Revolt in 1936.

The Arab Revolt began as a general strike called by Hajj Amin al-Husseini but grew into a violent movement that was to last through 1939, with participation by thousands of Palestinian Arabs. It resulted in bombings of infrastructure (such as railroads and government buildings) and attacks on both the British and the Jews. In the course of the revolt, al-Husseini brought together a coalition of all the major Palestinian parties under the umbrella of the Arab Higher Committee, which he led. The 1936 Arab Revolt also spurred the development of the Irgun Zvai Leumi, a militant breakaway group from the Haganah, the main Zionist defense force. An even more militant group broke away from the Irgun in 1940 to form Lehi, also known as the Stern Gang (for its founder Avraham Stern). Now there would be Jewish reprisals against Arabs, as well as instances of Jewish terrorism against both Arab and British targets, including the bombing by the Irgun of the King David Hotel (home to the British army headquarters) in 1946.

During the 1930s unrest in Palestine forced the British to modify their plans for the future of the mandate territory. (Opposite) A British riot squad disperses Arab rioters outside a government building in Jaffa. (Right) The fiery rhetoric of Grand Mufti Hajj Amin al-Husseini helped lead to the Arab Revolt of 1936–39.

3 *Two States for Two Nations?*

*T*he two nations living in Palestine—the Palestinians and the Jews— claimed the same land, and neither people wanted to be ruled by the other. So the British prime minister appointed a commission of distinguished people to study the problem, interview the conflicting parties, and make recommendations.

The immediate problem was the Arab Revolt in 1936. This Revolt, which ended in 1939, was triggered by a steep rise in Jewish immigration, mostly by Jews attempting to escape persecution in Nazi Germany. While the British sought to stem the revolt using military means, they also sought to resolve the problems that gave rise to the Revolt; hence, the establishment of the Peel Commission.

The Peel Commission's Proposal

The Peel Commission, headed by Lord William Wellesley Peel, was established in 1937 and in a few months set forth its view that the cultural and political differences between the two nations of Palestine were irreconcilable. They therefore recommended that the land be divided three ways, as shown on the map on page 39. A small area in the north of Palestine, representing about 20 percent of the territory, would be set aside for the Jewish state. Most of the rest of Palestine would be set aside for an Arab state that would exist in federation with Transjordan. Finally, Jerusalem, a city that was considered holy by three religions, would fall under international jurisdiction so that all the sacred places in and around the city might be protected and respected. (The British would also maintain control over a corridor between Jaffa and Jerusalem.) Under this plan, each nation would have to give up a portion of its claim to make room for the other nation. It is also envisaged a transfer of populations—Arabs out of the future Jewish state, and Jews out of the future Arab state—voluntarily if possible, compulsory if not.

The area for the Jewish state corresponded with the area where the vast majority of Jews lived, though it excluded Jerusalem, which had contained a Jewish majority since the mid-1800s. Since Jews represented just over a quarter of the population of Palestine in 1937, the state they were to be given was rather small. It was much less than what Jewish leaders wanted, or what they assumed they would need if many more Jews immigrated to the area. On the other hand, the Peel Commission's proposal was the first time the British government had explicitly envisaged a Jewish state, and not just a Jewish "homeland." In that sense the proposal represented a step forward so far as the Jews were concerned. Moreover, this was a time when the need for a safe place to live was becoming increasingly urgent as events in Nazi Germany unfolded.

Consequently, the Jews accepted the proposal in principle, subject to negotiating the borders of the proposed states and despite the opposition of some Zionists. A group known as the Revisionist Zionists believed that the British had already partitioned Palestine by creating Transjordan from the Palestine Mandate. (This was not really accurate, as Transjordan was never legally part of Palestine so far as the British or the League of Nations were concerned.) To the Revisionists the idea of further partitioning what was left of

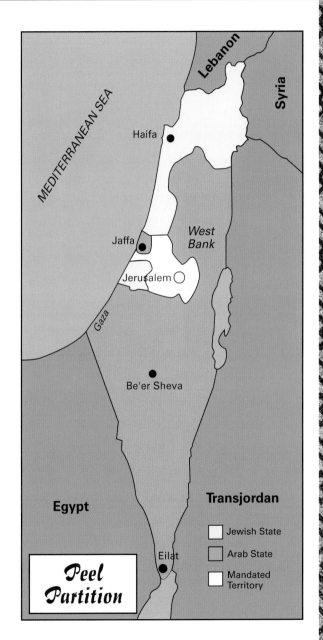

Palestine was totally unacceptable. Similarly, the Palestinian Arabs wanted no part of any partition, believing that no division of the land would be legitimate.

Zionist Views

Within the Zionist movement there were three different views or visions about the future of Palestine. The Revisionist Zionists, led by Vladimir Jabotinsky, supported a "Greater Israel," meaning a Jewish state in possession not only of Palestine up to the Jordan River but a state with sovereignty over both sides of the Jordan River. This included at least a strip of land on the east bank of the Jordan, and ideally most or all of Transjordan.

Vladimir Jabotinsky (1880–1940) believed that the Jewish state in Palestine should include territory on both banks of the Jordan River. His supporters became known as the Alliance of Revisionists-Zionists.

The second vision, a minimalist view, was that of a single binational state in all of Palestine in which Jews and Arabs shared power but in which the Jewish right to settle in the land was uncontested. This was the view of such Jewish thinkers as Judah Magnes and Martin Buber.

The third vision, upheld by mainstream Zionist leaders Chaim Weizmann and David Ben-Gurion and supported by a majority of the Zionist movement, was acceptance of a small Jewish state within part of Palestine, existing side by side with an Arab state in the rest of Palestine. Though the Zionist mainstream would have preferred to have all of Palestine (at least all of it to the west of the Jordan River), their leaders felt it was better to have a state—even a small one—than not to have one at all. Thus they decided to support a compromise.

The Palestinian side, however, did not accept the compromise. Palestinian politics was dominated by the Husseini family, and Hajj Amin al-Husseini refused to accept any Jewish state, even a small one. In his view, Palestine was Islamic holy land that could never be entrusted to non-Muslims. Thus the Palestinian side rejected partition out of hand, even though the partition plan called for a Jewish state far smaller than the one that exists

Chaim Weizmann (1874–1952) and other mainstream Zionist leaders were willing to compromise with the British in order to gain a Jewish state in Palestine. Weizmann later became the first president of Israel.

today. During the Arab Revolt, Hajj Amin al Husseini and his followers killed not only Jews and the British but Arab moderates as well.

Limits on Jewish Immigration

The British set up the Woodhead Commission to determine how best to implement the Peel recommendations, but it ended by reversing those recommendations altogether, as British leaders came to view partition as impractical. Then in 1939, with war clouds on the horizon, the British clamped down on Jewish immigration and effectively overturned the Balfour Declaration. Knowing that war with Nazi Germany was imminent, British leaders needed to end unrest in the empire and keep the Arabs on their side. They knew that the Jews had little choice but to side with the British.

The British policy was proclaimed in a 1939 White Paper, which explained:

> It has been the hope of British Governments ever since the Balfour Declaration was issued that in time the Arab population, recognizing the advantages to be derived from Jewish settlement and development in Palestine, would become reconciled to the further growth of the Jewish National Home. This hope has not been fulfilled.

The White Paper announced that Jewish immigration would be limited to 75,000 people over the next five years and that all subsequent immigration would be contingent upon Arab consent. (This provision would effectively end future Jewish immigration.) The White Paper also restricted the sale of land to Jews. Ten years down the line, it envisaged establishing an independent state in Palestine that would be neither Jewish nor Arab but binational.

While the Arabs were not entirely pleased with the White Paper, the Jews saw it as a complete betrayal. The two groups agreed on one issue, however: both wanted Britain out of Palestine. The Jews reacted to the White Paper by encouraging illegal immigration. But when World War II began in

September 1939 with Hitler's invasion of Poland, the Jews had little choice but to cooperate with the British in fighting the Nazis. This circumstance led Jewish leader David Ben-Gurion to urge Jews to aid the British in the war against the Nazis as if there were no White Paper, but to fight the British as if there were no war.

During the 1940s Germany's Nazi government planned and carried out a program to exterminate the Jews of Europe. (Opposite) The bodies of murdered Jews are piled onto a cart. Approximately 6 million Jews died during the Holocaust. (Right) Ovens in the crematorium at the Dachau Concentration Camp.

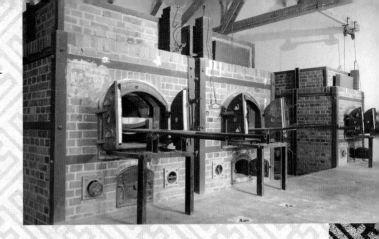

4 *The German War Against the Jewish Nation*

World War II began on September 1, 1939, but the German campaign against the Jews of Europe really began on January 30, 1933, with the election of Adolf Hitler as chancellor of the Third Reich. The Second World War began with small steps, as Hitler aimed to achieve *Lebensraum,* or "living room," for Germany, which had lost territory in World War I. He also sought to make Germany *Judenrein* (free of Jews) by making life so difficult for Jews that they would seek to live elsewhere. But over the course of seven or eight years, the harassment escalated and the goal changed from expelling the Jews from Germany to exterminating all the Jews of Europe.

Persecution of Jews Begins

In January 1933 the National Socialist German Workers' Party (Nationalsozialistische Deutsche Arbeiterpartei, NSDAP, or Nazi Party), won the largest share of popular votes in a democratic election. Though Hitler's hatred of the Jews was quite explicit in his widely read book *Mein Kampf*, which he wrote while in prison during 1924, many observers assumed he would be more moderate

German leader Adolf Hitler (1889–1945) salutes marching troops, circa 1937. After coming to power in Germany, Hitler and the Nazis systematically persecuted German Jews.

when in power. They were wrong. He quickly changed the German political system from a weak democratic republic to a strong dictatorship. At the same time, he enacted laws that persecuted the country's Jews, making it impossible for a Jew to earn a living in Germany.

The early steps, taken in April 1933, began with boycotts of Jewish businesses, then laws barring Jews from the civil service, then further laws barring Jews from other forms of employment. Signs bearing the warning "Jews not wanted" started popping up everywhere. In 1935, with the establishment of the Nuremberg Laws, Jews were stripped of their German citizenship. Random acts of violence against Jews became increasingly common. On November 9–10, 1938, there was a night of violence and vandalism against Jews, their homes, and their businesses in Germany and parts of Austria (which had been incorporated into Germany). This violence was similar to the pogroms in Russia during the late 1800s and early 1900s. It was called *Kristallnacht*, or the Night of Broken Glass.

A Nazi party member stands outside a Berlin store with a placard that reads, "Germans, protect yourselves! Do not buy from Jews." The boycott of Jewish businesses began in April 1933.

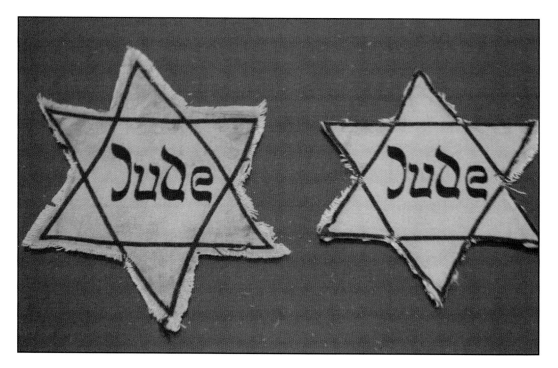

During the 1930s German laws required Jews to wear badges like these on their clothing, which identified them publicly as Jews.

By 1938 one quarter of Germany's 500,000 Jews had emigrated, many to Palestine. However, many others stayed in Germany—the land they had grown up in, fought for, and loved. Many German Jews had risen to prominence in the arts, education, and business, and they fully expected their fellow Germans to turn Hitler out of office. For those who did wish to leave there were many obstacles—the biggest being uncertainty over who would take them in. Even Palestine was not always the answer, because of increasing British restrictions on Jewish immigration into Palestine.

"No One Wants to Have Them"

In the summer of 1938, delegates from 32 countries, including the United States, met in Evian, France, to discuss the question of Jewish refugees leaving Germany and Austria. Few countries were willing to take in more Jews. The lesson of "the Jew conference in Evian," as the Nazi party newspaper *Voelkischer Beobachter* put it on July 13, 1938, was that "no one wants to have them."

This was soon proven by a series of incidents involving Jewish refugees from Germany. On May 13, 1939, some 800 Jews boarded the S.S. *St. Louis* in Hamburg to make a journey across the Atlantic to Cuba, where they hoped to stay until permitted to enter the United States. Most of them had lost their means of livelihood because of the increasing burden of Nazi regulations. They had to rely on contributions from family and friends abroad to pay the cost of the trip, as well as special fees mandated by the Nazi regime. However, upon landing in Cuba, the Jews were denied permission to stay. Since neither the United States nor other countries in the Western hemisphere would let them in, they were forced to make a return trip across the Atlantic, disembarking at Antwerp, Belgium. After some negotiation, Holland took in 181 of the refugees, France 224, Great Britain 228, and Belgium 214. World War II began only a few months later, and by June 1940 Germany had conquered most of Western Europe. As a result, most of the *St. Louis* refugees were deported to Nazi concentration camps, where most died as victims of the Holocaust, the German campaign to eliminate the Jews from Europe.

Jewish refugees on the S.S. *St. Louis* wave as the ship arrives at Antwerp, June 1939. Most of the people in this picture probably died during the Holocaust, as the United States and other countries in the Western Hemisphere refused to allow them to enter and they were forced to return to Europe.

Another ship, the *Struma*, set sail in December 1941 from the Romanian Black Sea port of Constanta with 769 European Jewish refugees aboard. It headed toward Palestine but was turned back at the order of the British Minister Lord Moyne. Incidents like these sent a clear message to the world's

Jews. The Jewish people needed a safe haven and they could not count on any other country to provide it. No other country was prepared to take in masses of Jews even in a time of great emergency—not even the United States. This left only one solution: the prospective State of Israel.

In 1942, the year after the United States entered World War II, Zionists met at the Biltmore Hotel in New York to set forth their demands—unrestricted Jewish immigration to Palestine and an end to the British Mandate. Both had the express aim of establishing a Jewish state. These recommendations became known as the Biltmore Program.

Holocaust Survivors

World War II ended in 1945. Germany had lost, and those of its leaders who were still alive faced the world's first war crimes trial as the extent of the Holocaust became known to the world. The Nazis had succeeded in killing off more than half of Europe's Jews and more than one-third of the world's Jews—6 million out of a global population of 15 million. (Today, there are 13 million Jews around the world. Eleven million live in two countries—the United States and Israel.)

When the war ended there was the matter of what to do with the surviving Jews. As late as the 1930s, Zionism was still only favored by a minority of the world's Jews, but after the Holocaust the need for a Jewish state was readily and tragically apparent to most Jews. Some 250,000 European Jews had been displaced from their homes as well as their countries and had to live in special camps for a year or more after the war. Many of these Jews had only one desire—to go to Palestine.

Three young Jewish survivors of the concentration camp at Buchenwald hold a homemade flag, June 1945. Like most other survivors, they hoped to make their way to Palestine after the war ended.

Under pressure from the Americans to admit more refugees into Palestine, the British agreed to establish the Anglo-American Committee of Inquiry. It was designed to study conditions in Palestine and the condition of Jewish refugees in Europe. The committee's findings underscored not only the tragedy of the Holocaust but the ongoing tragedy after the Holocaust, as well as the urgent need to open the doors to Palestine. In its recommendations, the Committee called on the British to let 100,000 Jewish immigrants into Palestine, while urging the rest of the world to provide space for the remaining Jewish refugees.

Despite the call for increased immigration into Palestine, this was no Zionist-inspired committee: it recommended against the establishment of a Jewish state in Palestine as well as against an Arab state. It envisaged two self-governing communities within one state and international protection for the holy places of three faiths, a proposition acceptable neither to the Palestinian Arabs nor to the Palestinian Jews.

Despite the recommendations of the Anglo-American Committee, Britain worked hard to prevent more Jews from entering Palestine. At the same time, Jews already in Palestine worked hard to get them in—sometimes by illegal means. In one famous incident, a ship set sail from France on July 11, 1947, with over 4,500 displaced persons aboard. These were Jewish Holocaust survivors whose homes in Europe no longer existed. Their destination was Palestine. As the ship approached Palestine, British forces boarded the ship. They met with some resistance but overcame it with force. The British then led the ship into port at Haifa and deported the passengers back to Europe, where they ended up in camps for displaced persons—in Germany. After this highly publicized incident, pressure mounted on the British to leave Palestine, which they eventually did, handing over the issue of the disposition of Palestine to the United Nations.

(Opposite) David Ben-Gurion declares Israel's independence in Tel Aviv, May 14, 1948. (Right) Members of the Israeli Defense Force stand around a British-made Egyptian fighter plane shot down during Israel's War for Independence. Although the Arabs possessed greater numbers and superior weapons, they were outfought by the tiny Jewish state.

5 *The Arab War Against the Jewish State*

Carrying out the responsibilities of the Palestine Mandate proved more costly and more difficult than the British had ever anticipated, particularly with the rise of both Jewish and Arab violence against British targets. Consequently, in February 1947 Britain announced it would turn over the Mandate to the United Nations, which was formed after the Second World War to replace the failed League of Nations. The United Nations set up a special commission to study the problem, the UN Special

Commission on Palestine. It consisted of 11 members, who considered a variety of options, including those recommended by the Jewish Agency and the Arab Higher Committee. The Jews proposed a Jewish state in all of Palestine while the Arabs proposed an Arab state in all of Palestine. Both ideas were ruled out for the obvious reason that to accept either one was to negate the rights and claims of the other side.

The UN Partition Plan

The Commission's work culminated in a majority proposal and a minority proposal. The minority proposed a single binational state governed by a federal government combining two relatively autonomous states into one. The majority proposal proposed a partition plan, much like that proposed by the Peel Commission. Like the Peel Partition Plan before it, the UN partition plan envisaged the division of Palestine into two states. Under this plan, Jerusalem would be established as a separate entity administered directly by the United Nations. In this plan, however, the Jewish state would occupy about 55 percent of the land area of Palestine while the Arab state would occupy about 45 percent (with the Jewish portion including the Negev Desert). The Jewish state was designed to accommodate not only all the Jews in Palestine, but also the many Jews who were still expected to emigrate from other parts of the world.

For the Revisionist Zionists, this partition plan, like the one before it, was still unacceptable, but the majority of Zionists accepted the plan. As Chaim Weizmann argued: "We realize that we cannot have the whole of Palestine. God made a promise: Palestine to the Jews. It is up to the Almighty to keep

His Promise. Our business is to do what we can in a very imperfect human way." For the Arabs, any partition was unacceptable. In their view, they constituted the majority of the population (1.2 million Arabs compared to 600,000 Jews), and should not have to accommodate Zionism or provide the solution to the problems of European Jews. The Arabs opposed both the majority and the minority plans, threatening war if either one were adopted.

The United Nations, which in 1947 consisted of 57 states, voted on November 29 to accept the partition plan. Thirty-three countries voted in favor of the resolution, while 13 voted against the plan and 10 abstained.

Both the United States and the Soviet Union, its World War II ally but now rival, voted in favor of partition, while Great Britain abstained. President Harry Truman instructed the US mission to the UN to vote in favor, despite contrary advice from his Secretary of State

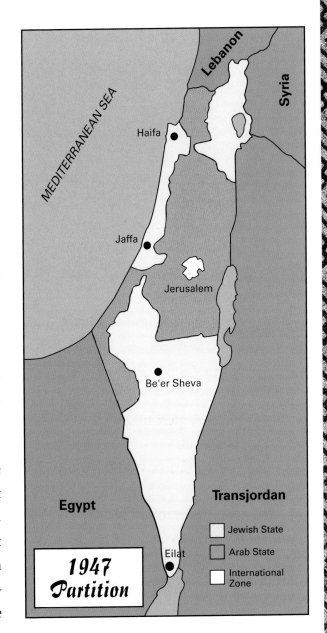

1947 Partition

Jewish State

Arab State

International Zone

and Secretary of Defense. Both feared antagonizing the Arab world and jeopardizing American oil interests in the region. Some have argued that Truman acted on the basis of domestic politics (pandering to the Jewish vote). Others say Truman's position was a matter of conscience, deriving from a religious conviction that Palestine belonged to the Jews and providing justice for the survivors of the Holocaust. The Soviet Union, whose interests over the next few decades were to run counter to those of the United States, voted in favor in order to weaken the British position in the Middle East.

A Violent Response

Violence broke out in Palestine overnight. Palestinian Arabs attacked Jews and Jews responded to those attacks. Arabs also assaulted Jews in cities across the Arab world, a tragic confirmation that Jews did indeed need a place they could call their own. For the first few months, the tide was running against the Jews, and few observers expected the Jews to succeed in establishing a state. But in March 1948 the Haganah went on the offensive to capture Arab towns as well as key roads and heights.

In the course of the violence, both sides committed atrocities. In April 1948 the Irgun and the Stern Gang massacred some 250 Palestinian villagers living in Deir Yassin. Menachem Begin, one of the Irgun leaders (and a future prime minister of Israel), argued that the village was being used as a headquarters by Arab terrorists; others insist that those killed were innocent civilians. Whatever the truth, it has been argued by many that this event stimulated the exodus of Palestinian Arabs from Palestine, and was part of an Israeli plan to expel all Palestinians from the region. These points are also debated. Researchers have pored through Israeli archives but have found no plan to expel the Arabs. Indeed there were not only instances in which Jewish officials publicly called on Palestinian Arabs to stay put, there was also a secret directive issued by the Haganah National Command to all units to secure the rights of Arabs in the Jewish state. In addition, in war it is quite typical for people to flee, especially if they expect their side to eventually triumph, permitting a safe return.

A few days after the events at Deir Yassin, Palestinian Arabs massacred 80 Jewish doctors, nurses, university professors, and students traveling to Jerusalem in a medical convoy. This episode, lasting several hours, occurred just a short distance away from a British military post, but the British solders that were supposed to keep peace in Palestine made no attempt to intervene.

Independence and War

On May 14, 1948, the day the British Mandate officially ended, David Ben-Gurion proclaimed the new State of Israel in a ceremony that took place at the Tel Aviv Museum. The next day five Arab states attacked the newborn state, and what began as a war between Palestinian Arabs and Palestinian Jews became an Arab-Israeli war. Just three years after the end of the Holocaust, the Arab states settled on a plan to extinguish the Jewish state.

Israel was heavily outnumbered. The combined populations of the five warring Arab states—Egypt, Syria, Jordan, Lebanon, and Iraq—was 50 times that of Israel. The Arabs also possessed superior weaponry and equipment. In the first two weeks of the war the Arab side had more than 70 combat aircraft

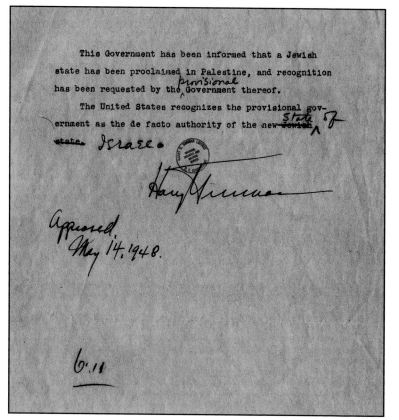

This Government has been informed that a Jewish state has been proclaimed in Palestine, and recognition has been requested by the *provisional* Government thereof.

The United States recognizes the provisional government as the de facto authority of the new *State of* ~~Jewish~~ ~~state.~~ *Israel.*

Harry Truman

Approved.
May 14, 1948.

6:11

The United States was the first country to officially recognize the State of Israel. This is a draft copy of President Harry S. Truman's remarks, which he made the evening of May 14, 1948—11 minutes after the British mandate for Palestine officially expired.

while Israel had none. In addition the Israelis had but two tanks, and only one had a gun. The Arab side held massive military superiority, eased eventually—but only in part—by Soviet-approved sales of arms by Czechoslovakia to the Israelis, and to a lesser extent by French arms sales. The United States had declared an arms embargo on both sides. The British honored its prior arms agreements with Iraq and Transjordan, and a British soldier commanded Transjordan's Arab Legion, the best-trained force in the region.

However, despite attempts to coordinate strategy among the Arabs, there was very little coordination. Each Arab state had its own agenda, and those agendas did not necessarily coincide with the Palestinian Arab agenda. In 1947 and 1948 King Abdullah of Transjordan (the great-grandfather of the current King Abdullah of Jordan) held secret talks with the Israeli emissary (and future prime minister) Golda Meir. At that meeting Abdullah agreed to limit his objectives in the coming war to territory set aside in the UN partition for a West Bank Arab state. He also agreed to leave alone the territory set aside for the Jewish state. The two sides, however, both coveted Jerusalem, which was to be set aside as an international zone. So far as Abdullah was concerned, the Grand Mufti of Jerusalem was his enemy; hence his willingness to deal with the Israelis. (In 1951, King Abdullah was assassinated by followers of the Grand Mufti as he was leaving prayers at the Al Aqsa Mosque, with his grandson, the future King Hussein, at his side.)

For Syria, the purpose of the war was to take back what its leaders felt was rightfully part of Syria. At a minimum the Syrians wanted to take control over the northern part of Palestine. For Egypt, the purpose was the need to be seen as participant in the war against the interlopers and to prevent other Arab states from seizing territory in Palestine.

Armistice Agreements

As for the new State of Israel, it too had its share of division. In June 1948 an Irgun ship bearing the name *Altalena* (the pen name for Revisionist leader Vladimir Jabotinsky) was delivering arms for Israel, but the Irgun intended to keep a portion of the arms for its own use rather than handing them over

FA/19/48

מדינת ישראל
הממשלה הזמנית
STATE OF ISRAEL
PROVISIONAL GOVERNMENT
MINISTRY FOR FOREIGN AFFAIRS

Hakirya,
6th August,1948.

Count Folke Bernadotte,
United Nations Mediator.

Sir,

In confirmation of my oral statement to you at
our meeting yesterday, I beg to request, on behalf of
the Provisional Government of Israel, that you be kind
enough to transmit to the Governments of the Arab States
now at war with Israel our offer that their representatives
should meet the representatives of the Provisional
Government of Israel for the purpose of peace negotiations.

The Provisional Government would be grateful for
the earliest possible communication of the Arab Governments'
replies to this proposal.

I am,

Yours faithfully,
M. Shertok
MINISTER FOR FOREIGN AFFAIRS

MS/rh

to the Israel Defense Force. In the belief that the new state of Israel should have but one unified military, Ben-Gurion ordered Colonel (and future prime minister) Yitzhak Rabin to fire on the ship and sink it, which he did. Irgun leader Menachem Begin (another future prime minister) was on the ship but managed to make it to safety.

(Opposite) A letter from Israel's foreign minister to UN mediator Count Folke Bernadotte, requesting peace negotiations. (Right) Bernadotte (center) was assassinated by Jewish extremists after proposing a peace plan that would have required Israel to give up its independence. After the assassination, a period began called "the Hunting Season," in which the Haganah aided the British in capturing members of the Stern Gang and the Irgun.

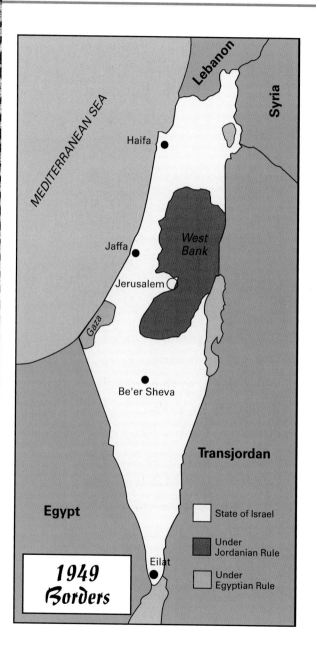

MEDITERRANEAN SEA

Lebanon

Syria

Haifa

Jaffa

West Bank

Jerusalem

Gaza

Be'er Sheva

Transjordan

Egypt

State of Israel

Under Jordanian Rule

Under Egyptian Rule

Eilat

1949 Borders

In the course of the fighting, the United Nations put in place a series of ceasefires that did not hold. During one ceasefire the UN mediator and Swedish diplomat Count Folke Bernadotte laid out a plan that resembled the minority plan originally put forth by the UN Commission on Palestine a year earlier. In effect, it asked Israel to give up the independence it had successfully defended. The plan proved to be unacceptable both to the Israelis and to the Arabs. In September, members of the Stern Gang murdered Bernadotte.

By the war's end, the Israelis had suffered 6,000 dead out of a population of 650,000, or 1 percent of the population. Arab losses are uncertain, but some estimate the loss of 8,000 Palestinians, and 4,000 other Arabs. Separate armistice agreements, rather than peace treaties— an armistice suspends a state of war but does not end it—were signed between Israel and Egypt, Lebanon, Transjordan, and Syria between February and July

1949. (Iraq did not sign an armistice agreement.) These agreements, negotiated on the island of Rhodes under the auspices of UN mediator Ralph Bunche, left Israel with control over 78 percent of Palestine (including West Jerusalem) rather than the 55 percent awarded in the UN partition plan. However, the other 22 percent did not become a separate Palestinian Arab state: the West Bank and East Jerusalem (and with it, the Western Wall) were simply incorporated into Transjordan, which then became the Hashemite Kingdom of Jordan, while Gaza was occupied by Egypt.

Israelis refer to the 1948–1949 conflict as the War of Independence; the Palestinians refer to it as the *nahkba* (Arabic for catastrophe). As a result of the war, about 750,000 Palestinian Arabs fled Palestine. In the ensuing years a similar number of Jews fled other Arab countries in the Middle East and came to Israel, where they were absorbed into the general population. Of the 750,000 Palestinians who fled, a few became citizens of Jordan. However, other Arab states refused to offer these Arabs citizenship, so they remained refugees in Lebanon, Syria, Gaza, and Egypt. On January 25, 1949, Israel held its first national election for the 120-seat Constituent Assembly (later called the Knesset). Ben-Gurion's Mapai party won a plurality of votes but not a majority, so he formed Israel's first coalition government. On March 11, 1949, the United Nations approved Israel's application for membership, and the new state officially joined the UN in May of that year.

In September 1993 it seemed the Israeli-Palestinian dispute might end peacefully after a historic agreement between Israel's Prime Minister Yitzhak Rabin and Yasir Arafat's Palestine Liberation Organization. However, the peace process collapsed seven years later. (Right) Palestinian militants like these continue to attack Israel, and refuse to accept the state's right to exist.

6 Epilogue: The Return of the Two-State Solution

Six decades after the State of Israel was established, the two nations—Palestinians and Israelis—still stand apart. Unrest has continued in the region, with a series of conflicts between Israel and its Arab neighbors (1956, 1967, 1973, and 1982), two *intifadas* ("uprisings") among the Palestinians (1987, 2000), peace treaties with Egypt (1979) and Jordan (1994), and a collapsed agreement with Palestinian leaders (1993).

Palestinians walk past a controversial security barrier currently being constructed around Israel's territory, including some settlements in the West Bank. Israeli leaders say the barrier is necessary to protect citizens from terrorist attacks.

The Palestinian Authority, which has governed the Palestinian territories since 1993 under the terms of the Oslo Agreement between Israel and the Palestinians, is deeply divided. One faction, Fatah, appears to be willing to acknowledge Israel's right to exist and favors a negotiated settlement. Another faction, Hamas, has not renounced terrorism, and its charter calls for the destruction of the state of Israel. Its leaders believe that "historic Palestine" can never be divided.

Within Israel, a small minority exists that does not accept the Palestinians' right to a state of their own but they are small in number and wield no power.

In July 2000 U.S. President Bill Clinton met with then-Prime Minister Ehud Barak of Israel and then-chairman of the Palestinian Authority Yasir Arafat to bring about a peace treaty that would allow the establishment of a Palestinian state side by side with Israel. In that summit meeting and in meetings that followed in December, the Palestinians were offered all of Gaza, most of the West Bank, and part of Jerusalem. However, the meetings foundered on the issue of refugees, the status of Jerusalem, and borders.

It seems likely that, if there ever is peace between the Israelis and the Palestinians, it will approximate what was offered in 2000—which has parallels with the two-state solution first proposed in 1937 by the British, then again in 1947 by the United Nations. Many wars have been fought and many lives have been lost but there is still the chance that in the end two states will one day live side by side in peace, recognizing as Chaim Weizmann once said, that the clash between Israelis and Palestinians is between two rights rather than between right and wrong.

1882: The first *aliyah*, or wave of Jewish immigration into Palestine, begins. Most of the immigrants are seeking to escape persecution in the Russian Empire or Eastern Europe.

1897: Theodor Herzl organizes the First Zionist Congress at Basel, Switzerland, and proposes the establishment of a national homeland for the Jews.

1914: World War I begins in August, pitting the Central Powers (Germany, Austria-Hungary, and the Ottoman Empire) against the Allies (Britain, France, and Russia).

1915: Sir Henry McMahon, the British high commissioner in Egypt, begins a correspondence with Sharif Hussein of Mecca, in which he promises independence for the Arabs if they will revolt against the Ottoman Turks.

1916: With the secret Sykes-Picot Agreement, Britain and France agree to divide the Middle East into spheres of influence.

1917: British Foreign Secretary Arthur James Balfour issues a letter declaring Britain's support for the establishment of a "national home for the Jewish people" in Palestine; in December British troops, assisted by their Arab allies, capture Jerusalem.

1918: The First World War ends with Britain in control of Palestine.

1919: Delegates to the Paris Peace Conference agree to establish the League of Nations, an international organization intended to prevent future wars by permitting nations to resolve disagreements through diplomacy and negotiation. Rather than granting outright independence to the Arabs, or creating the promised Jewish homeland, the League of Nation divides the Arab lands into new countries and places them under either British or French control. Great Britain is granted the mandate for Palestine.

1920: In March the General Syrian Congress elects Faisal, son of Sharif Hussein of Mecca, as king of Greater Syria, a territory that includes the modern states of Syria, Lebanon, Jordan, and Israel as well as the West Bank and Gaza; anti-Zionists riot in Jerusalem in April; at the San Remo Conference, Britain is assigned the mandate to control Palestine; in June, the Jewish Self-Defense Force Haganah is organized by Vladimir Jabotinsky; in July France evicts Faisal from Syria, and Britain names Herbert Samuel as High Commissioner of Palestine.

1921: At the Cairo conference in March, the British name Faisal king of Iraq while his brother, Abdullah, is named emir of the new British mandate of Transjordan; anti-Zionist riots take place in Jaffa in May; Hajj Amin al-Husseini, a member of an influential Palestinian family, is appointed Grand Mufti of Jerusalem.

1922: The Churchill White Paper is released in June; the Council of the League of Nations officially assigns the Palestine Mandate to Britain in July.

1923: The British Mandate for Palestine officially comes into force in September.

1929: Anti-Jewish riots take place in Jerusalem, Hebron, and elsewhere.

1930: In October Sir John Hope Simpson issues a report recommending the cessation of Jewish immigration to Palestine.

1933: In January Adolf Hitler becomes chancellor of Germany.

1936: Increased immigration of Jews to Palestine triggers the Arab Revolt, which lasts until 1939.

1937: The Peel Commission Report proposes partition of Palestine into Jewish and Arab states.

1939: A British White Paper calls for restricting Jewish immigration to Palestine, in an effort to appease the Arabs and end unrest in the British Empire; World War II begins when Germany invades Poland in September.

1945: As Allied forces march through Germany at the end of World War II, liberating concentration camps, the extent of the Holocaust is revealed. Ultimately, some 6 million European Jews were killed by the Nazis.

1946: The Anglo-American Committee of Inquiry report proposes that 100,000 Jewish immigrants be allowed to enter Palestine; in July, the Irgun and Stern Gang bomb Jerusalem's King David Hotel, which serves as the British headquarters in Palestine. The bombing is the deadliest attack against the British in the history of the Mandate.

1947: In November, the United Nations approves a resolution to partition Palestine into Jewish and Arab states.

1948: On May 14 the British Mandate ends, and Israel declares its independence. The next day war between Israel and its Arab neighbors begins.

1949: Israel signs armistice agreements with Jordan, Egypt, Lebanon, and Syria.

aliyah—immigration of Jews to Israel; the Hebrew word literally means "going up."

Balfour Declaration—an official British proclamation, issued in November 1917, that promised a Jewish national home in Palestine.

Eretz Yisrael—Hebrew for "Land of Israel."

Haganah—established in 1920 as a self-defense force for the Jewish settlers of Palestine; upon the establishment of the State of Israel, it became the Israel Defense Force.

Histadrut—the labor union federation in Palestine founded in 1920 that became a cornerstone of the economy.

Hussein-McMahon Correspondence—an exchange of 10 letters during 1915 and 1916 between Sharif Hussein of Mecca and the British High Commissioner in Egypt concerning the future status of the Middle East.

Irgun—a Revisionist paramilitary movement that broke away from the Haganah.

League of Nations—an international organization established at the Paris Peace Conference of 1919 to settle international disputes; it was a predecessor to the United Nations.

Lehi—a Revisionist paramilitary movement that broke away from the Irgun; also known as the Stern Gang.

mandate—responsibility granted by the League of Nations to administer a territory.

Peel Commission—British commission headed by Lord Peel that proposed partition in Palestine in 1937.

San Remo Conference—an international conference of the victorious powers in World War I that determined the allocation of mandates of former Ottoman lands.

Sykes-Picot Agreement——a 1916 agreement between France and England defining their spheres of influence in the Middle East.

White Papers——statements of policy issued by the British Government.

Zionism—— the Jewish national movement to establish a homeland or state in Palestine.

Antonius, George. *The Arab Awakening: The Story of the Arab National Movement*. Phoenix, Ariz.: Simon Publications, 2001.

Carew-Miller, Anna. *The Palestinians*. Philadelphia: Mason Crest Publishers, 2004.

Fromkin, David. *A Peace to End All Peace: The Fall of the Ottoman Empire and the Creation of the Modern Middle East*. New York: Avon Books, 1990.

Garfinkle, Adam. *Israel*. Philadelphia: Mason Crest Publishers, 2004.

Gilbert, Martin. *Atlas of the Arab-Israeli Conflict*. 6th ed. London: Routledge, 2003.

Laqueur, Walter, and Barry Rubin, eds. *The Israel-Arab Reader*. 6th ed. New York: Penguin Books, 2001.

O'Brien, Conor Cruise. *The Siege*. New York: Simon and Schuster, 1986.

Scheindlin, Raymond P. *A Short History of the Jewish People: From Legendary Times to Modern Statehood.* New York: Oxford University Press, 1998.

Sykes, Christopher. *Crossroads to Israel, 1917–1948*. Bloomington: Indiana University Press, 1965.

Wasserstein, Bernard. *Israelis and Palestinians: Why Do They Fight? Can They Stop?* 2nd ed. New Haven: Yale University Press, 2004.

Internet Resources

http://www.yale.edu/lawweb/avalon/mideast/mideast.htm

The Web site of the Avalon Project at Yale Law School provides numerous primary source documents pertaining to events in the Middle East from 1916 to the present.

http://www.fordham.edu/halsall/mod/modsbook54.html

The Internet Modern History Sourcebook Project is a collection of thousands of historical texts, including dozens on the Middle East from 1914 to the present.

http://www.jewishvirtuallibrary.org

The Jewish Virtual Library, sponsored by the American-Israeli Cooperative Enterprise, provides historical background, maps, primary documents, and other information pertaining to Judaism, Jewish history, ancient and modern Israel, and other related topics.

http://www.mideastweb.org/index.html

Mideast Web was started by people active in Middle East dialogue and peace education efforts. The Web site contains articles, commentaries, maps, and historic and current information on the countries and people of the Middle East.

Numbers in **bold italic** refer to captions.

Index

Contributors

Alan H. Luxenberg is vice president of the Foreign Policy Research Institute, one of the nation's oldest and most prestigious think tanks. He is also founder and director of FPRI's Marvin Wachman Fund for International Education, which seeks to foster civic and international literacy in the community and in the classroom.

Picture Credits